Geology Rocks!

Crystals

EXPRESS EDITION

Rebecca Faulkner

Raintree

Chicago, Illinois

Editorial: Kathryn Walker, Melanie Waldron, and
Rachel Howells
Design: Victoria Bevan, Rob Norridge,
and AMR Design Ltd (www.amrdesign.com)
Illustrations: David Woodroffe
Picture Research: Melissa Allison
Production: Duncan Gilbert
Originated by Chroma Graphics Pte. Ltd
Printed and bound in China by
South China Printing Company

12 11 10 09 08
10 9 8 7 6 5 4 3 2 1

**Library of Congress Cataloging-in-Publication
Data**
Faulkner, Rebecca.
   Crystals / Rebecca Faulkner.
      p. cm. -- (Geology Rocks)
   Includes bibliographical references and index.
   ISBN-13: 978-1-4109-2775-0 (lib. bdg.)
   ISBN-10: 1-4109-2775-X (lib. bdg.)
   ISBN-13: 978-1-4109-2783-5 (pbk.)
   ISBN-10: 1-4109-2783-0 (pbk.)
   1. Crystals--Juvenile literature. I. Title.
   QD906.3.F39 2008
   548--dc22
                                    2006037064

This leveled text is a version of *Freestyle:
Geology Rocks: Crystals*.

Acknowledgments
The publishers would like to thank the following for
permission to reproduce photographs:

©Alamy p. **25** (Arco Images), pp. **5 top inset,
42** (BE&W), p. **16** (Cassida Images), p. **40** (Doug
Steley), pp. **5 bottom inset, 8** (Phototake Inc.),
p. **29 top** (Roger Cracknell), p. **34** (Scenics &
Science); ©Bridgeman Art Library p. **41** (Smithsonian
Institution, Washington DC, USA); ©Corbis
pp. **6, 18, 31, 33, 36 amethyst, 36 clear**, p. **7**
(Jose Manuel Sanchis Calvete), p. **43** (Alison Wright);
©Gavin Newman p. **4-5**; ©GeoScience Features
Picture Library pp. **12 quartz, 13, 24, 29 bottom,
35, 36 milky, 36 rose, 36 smoky, 38, 39**, p. **12
feldspar** (Prof. B. Booth), pp. **12 hornblende, 12
mica** (Visual Unlimited); ©Harcourt Education Ltd.
pp. **19, 22-23** (Tudor Photography); ©Photolibrary.
com p. **32**; ©Science Photo Library p. **11** (Charles
D. Winters), p. **17** (Colin Cuthbert), p. **44** (Dirk
Wiersma), p. **20** (Martin Bond), p. **37** (Martin Land),
p. **9 bottom** TIPS p. **28** (Guido Alberto Rossi);
©Visuals Unlimited pp. **12 center, 27 bottom**
(Doug Sokell), p. **26** (Dr. Ken Wagner), p. **30**
(Dr. Marli Miller), pp. **14, 21** (Mark A. Schneider)

Cover photograph of quartz reproduced with
permission of ©Science Photo Library (Simon Fraser).

Every effort has been made to contact copyright
holders of any material reproduced in this book.
Any omissions will be rectified in subsequent
printings if notice is given to the publishers.

Disclaimer
All the Internet addresses (URLs) given in this book
were valid at the time of going to press. However,
due to the dynamic nature of the Internet, some
addresses may have changed, or sites may have
changed or ceased to exist since publication. While
the author and publishers regret any inconvenience
this may cause readers, no responsibility for any
such changes can be accepted by either the author
or the publishers.

CONTENTS

Some words are printed in bold, **like this.** You can find out what they mean by looking in the glossary. You can also look for them in the **On The Rocks!** section at the bottom of each page.

GLITTERING CRYSTALS

Crystals are all around us. They are in rocks and riverbeds. They are in the sand on beaches. They are even in jewelry shops.

Crystals are shapes that **minerals** form when they grow. Minerals are solid materials found in nature. Rocks are made up of minerals.

➪ **This is Lechuguilla cave. It is in the state of New Mexico. This huge cave contains some amazing crystals.**

mineral   substance found in nature. Rocks are made from lots of minerals.

Crystals come in all shapes and sizes. Some are as large as a house. Others are too tiny to see.

Some crystals are very common. The salt in your kitchen is a common crystal. Others are rarer. They are harder to find.

Diamonds, rubies, and sapphires are used in jewelry. These are rare crystals. They take millions of years to form. Most crystals are smaller and form more quickly.

Find out later...

...how dentists use diamonds.

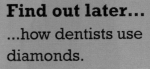

...how crystals can keep time.

...which crystal we eat.

WHAT ARE CRYSTALS?

Minerals are the materials that make up rock. Each mineral is made up of tiny pieces called **atoms**.

Some minerals are made from just one type of atom. For example, the mineral diamond is made only of carbon atoms.

Atoms in a mineral are arranged in special patterns. These special patterns are called **lattices**. As a

⇨ Rocks are made of minerals. Minerals come in lots of colors, sizes, and shapes.

mineral grows, the lattice repeats itself. This gives the mineral a shape. The shape is called a crystal.

Each mineral always grows into the same type of crystal. Its crystals are all made of the same type of atoms. For example, all quartz crystals contain silicon and oxygen atoms. They always grow as six-sided columns.

Flat faces
Crystals have flat, smooth sides. These are called **crystal faces.**

⇩ **These are crystals of the mineral galena. They grow in cube shapes. These crystals have six sides.**

crystal face

lattice three-dimensional pattern or arrangement. Three-dimensional means it has length, width, and depth.

Which crystals do you know?

Crystals are very important in our daily lives. Many of the things we use every day are made from crystals. There are crystals in watches and computers. There are even crystals in toothpaste.

You can find crystals all over your home. There are halite (salt) crystals in your saltshaker. The glasses you drink from are made from quartz crystals.

Crystals in toothpaste
You use crystals to brush your teeth. Toothpaste contains several types of crystals.

➩ **These are salt crystals that you can add to food.**

Watches use quartz crystals to keep time. Quartz crystals vibrate (shake) at a steady speed. They do this when a battery sends power through the crystal. The crystal's vibration keeps time in your watch.

Many crystals have bright colors. These can be ground up into powder. These powders give colors to paint.

⬅ **Watches use quartz crystals to keep the time.**

⮕ **This is a microchip. Microchips power computers. They are made from quartz crystals.**

CRYSTALS ALL OVER EARTH

Tiny crystals everywhere
The rocks of Earth's crust are made from crystals. We cannot always see these crystals. Many of them are too small to see.

Most crystals form from hot melted rock. This liquid rock is called **magma**. Crystals form as magma cools and hardens. It forms rock. This usually happens deep inside Earth.

Earth is made up of different layers. The **crust** is the thinnest layer. It is like Earth's skin. There are two types of crust. There are continental and

mantle

outer core

inner core

crust

⇨ **The outer layer of Earth is called the crust. It is made of different types of rock.**

oceanic crusts. Continental crust is beneath land. Oceanic crust is beneath oceans.

Below the crust is the **mantle**. This layer is about 1,800 miles (2,900 kilometers) deep.

The **core** is at the center of Earth. There is a solid inner core and a liquid outer core. The inner core is made of hard metal. The outer core is melted metal.

Melting rock
Temperatures in the mantle are up to 5,500° Fahrenheit (3,000° Celsius). In places the rocks are partly melted.

This is an olivine crystal. Olivine crystals form in Earth's mantle. It is very unusual to find them on Earth's surface.

mantle   hot layer of Earth beneath the crust

Rock types

Earth's **crust** (top layer) is made up of three groups of rock:

- igneous rocks
- sedimentary rocks
- metamorphic rocks.

Igneous rocks

Igneous rocks are formed from **magma**. This is hot melted rock. It is found in Earth's **mantle** (see page 7). Magma rises up through Earth's crust. As it rises it cools and hardens into igneous rock.

Rock recipes

Rocks are made up of materials called **minerals**. The crystals of different minerals grow and join together. They create different types of rock.

quartz

feldspar

mica

hornblende

⬇ **This is the igneous rock granite. It contains crystals of four minerals. These minerals are quartz, mica, feldspar, and hornblende crystals.**

Sedimentary rocks

Sedimentary rocks are formed from bits of other rocks. Rain or wind breaks off tiny pieces of rock. Wind or rivers carry them to a new place. These pieces pile up to form sedimentary rock.

Metamorphic rocks

Metamorphic rocks are rocks changed by heating and squashing. When magma rises it heats up the surrounding rocks. Sometimes Earth's crust moves. This squashes and folds rocks. The heated and squashed rocks become metamorphic rocks.

⬇ These are large crystals of garnet. These beautiful crystals are sometimes found in metamorphic rocks.

metamorphic rock   rock formed when igneous or sedimentary rocks are changed by heat or pressure

Crystals on the move

Most crystals form deep inside Earth. But in some places, they appear at the surface. They appear where the soil and rocks above are worn away.

On Earth rocks are formed, broken down, and formed again. This happens all the time. It is known as the **rock cycle**.

Over time even the hardest rocks are worn away. Wind and rain wear them away. This is called **weathering**. The rocks are broken down into clumps of crystals.

⬇ **This is a topaz crystal. Large crystals like this have been found in the countries of Russia and Brazil.**

These broken pieces of crystal are very small. They are carried away to different places. Wind, rivers, or ice carry them. The wearing away and removal of rock is called **erosion**.

Hard crystals can stand up to weathering and erosion. Many valuable crystals are very hard. These include diamonds and sapphires. They are worn away from rocks. But they are not destroyed.

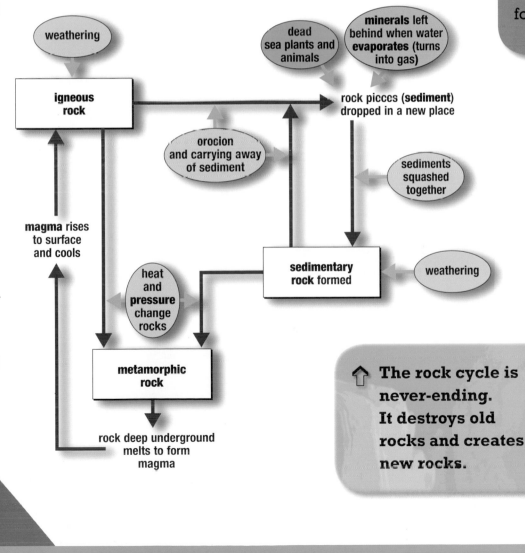

The rock cycle is never-ending. It destroys old rocks and creates new rocks.

CRYSTALS UNDER THE MICROSCOPE

Studying crystals
Scientists who study crystals are known as **crystallographers**.

Many crystals are very small. They can only be seen under a **microscope**. A microscope makes things look bigger.

Scientists cut thin slices of rock. They look at these pieces of rock under a microscope. They can then see the different crystals in the rock. They can see how the crystals fit tightly together.

⇨ **This is a very thin slice of rock seen under a microscope. The microscope makes the crystals appear brightly colored.**

microscope device used to see very small objects. It makes them appear bigger.

Scientists use a special type of microscope to do this. This is called a petrological microscope. The word petrological has to do with the study of rocks. This microscope can magnify rocks up to 2,000 times.

⇩ **This is an electron microscope. It allows scientists to see amazing detail in crystals.**

The electron microscope
Sometimes crystals are too small to see with a petrological microscope. Then an electron microscope is used. This can magnify crystals up to 1 million (1,000,000) times.

What's inside a crystal?

Crystals are made up of tiny parts called **atoms**. There are many ways that atoms can be arranged in crystals. They are arranged in patterns called **lattices**.

The same atoms can form different patterns. Heat and **pressure** can make them do this. Pressure is weight pressing against something.

For example, carbon crystals may form deep inside Earth. There is great heat and pressure there. These crystals may form diamonds.

⇩ **The atoms in a crystal are stacked together. They are stacked in a special order, like these tomatoes.**

lattice   three-dimensional pattern or arrangment. Three-dimensional means it has length, width, and depth.

Carbon crystals may also form nearer Earth's surface. There is less heat and pressure there. These crystals may form graphite.

The carbon atoms in graphite are arranged in layers. These layers can slide across each other. This makes graphite soft. It splits easily. In a diamond the carbon atoms are tightly packed. They are arranged in a strong lattice. This makes a diamond very hard.

Polymorphism
Graphite and diamond are **polymorphs** of carbon. This means they both contain the same atoms. But the atoms have joined together in different ways. Heat and pressure can cause this to happen.

⇨ **Diamond (right) and graphite (above) are both made of carbon atoms. The atoms have formed different crystals.**

polymorph   minerals that contain the same atoms, but have their atoms arranged in different ways.

How Do I Look?

Minerals are the solid materials that make up rock. A crystal is the shape that a mineral grows in. Each mineral forms crystals with a special shape.

Crystal systems

Crystal shapes can be divided into six groups. These are called **crystal systems**.

Each crystal system can have different shapes. But these shapes form in a similar way. They have similar features.

⬇ These are pyrite crystals. They are cubic crystals.

Cubic crystals

Crystals of the cubic system are often shaped like cubes (blocks). These have six **crystal faces** (flat sides). But there are many other crystal shapes in the cubic system. Some have eight faces. Some have ten. The minerals pyrite and diamond form cubic crystals.

Tetragonal crystals

Tetragonal crystals are often long shapes with four sides. They may have **pyramids** at each end. Pyramids are shapes made by sloping triangles. The mineral rutile forms tetragonal crystals.

Salt crystals
A salt crystal is shaped like a cube. Halite (rock salt) crystals belong to the cubic system.

pyramid shape

This is a crystal of rutile. It is a tetragonal crystal.

crystal face flat side of a crystal

Monoclinic system

Monoclinic is the most common group of crystal shapes. These crystals are often short and stubby. They have sloping **crystal faces** (flat sides) at each end. The **mineral** gypsum forms monoclinic crystals.

Hexagonal/trigonal system

The hexagonal and trigonal systems are very alike. Hexagonal crystals have six sides. Trigonal crystals have only three sides. The minerals apatite and quartz belong to this group.

Strange forms

Every crystal is different. This is because crystals usually grow slightly out of shape in some way.

topaz

gypsum

Orthorhombic system

Crystals of the orthorhombic system are usually short and stubby. Some of these crystals look a little like small rectangular boxes. Topaz crystals belong to this group.

Triclinic system

Triclinic is the most unusual group of crystals. They are usually flat with sharp edges. Triclinic crystals can have strange shapes. Turquoise crystals belong to this group.

These are the minerals topaz, gypsum, apatite, and quartz. Their crystals look very different.

apatite

quartz

Crystal habit

The **crystal systems** are the ways that a single crystal grows. But crystals do not usually grow alone. Many grow together. The way that crystals grow and fit together is called the **crystal habit**.

The **minerals** serpentine and asbestos form threadlike crystals. We say they have a fibrous habit.

Blocks and tables

Some crystals look like building blocks. We say they have a blocky habit. Some are flat, like a table. We say these have a tabular habit.

⬇ **This spiky mineral is called stibnite. Its crystals look like needles. We say they are acicular.**

The mineral natrolite has crystals that look like needles. We call this an acicular habit.

Crystals of malachite often have mammilated or botryoidal habits. A mammilated habit is when the crystals are like rounded lumps. A botryoidal habit is when they look like a bunch of grapes.

> ⇩ **This is a crystal of hematite. It has a kidney shape. This is called a reniform habit.**

Crystal shapes

Some common shapes of crystals are:

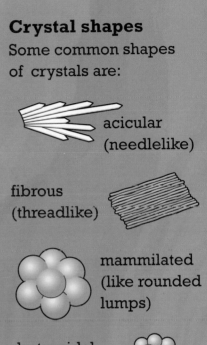

acicular (needlelike)

fibrous (threadlike)

mammilated (like rounded lumps)

botryoidal (like a bunch of grapes)

HOW DO CRYSTALS GROW?

Grow your own crystals

You can grow your own salt crystals at home. There are lots of crystal-growing kits you can buy. You can also find recipes for growing crystals on the Internet.

A crystal starts off very small. It grows as **atoms** (tiny parts) are added to it. The atoms repeat the crystal pattern. They repeat it in all directions. Two crystals of the same **mineral** can have the same shape. This happens if they can both grow freely.

But crystals are not usually free to grow in all directions. They often grow with other crystals. Then the crystals join together. They grow in a mixture of shapes.

⇨ **These are gypsum crystals. They form as water dries out in desert areas.**

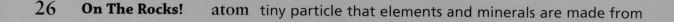

There are two main ways that crystals grow:

- in **magma** (hot melted rock)
- in water.

Most crystals grow deep inside Earth. They form when magma cools. Other crystals form from water that contains dissolved minerals. The minerals have broken down and mixed with the water.

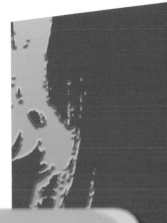

⬇ This is a type of rock called granite. Its crystals formed deep inside Earth.

Growth in water

Crystals can form when water **evaporates** (turns into gas). Water contains materials known as **minerals**. The water turns into steam. The minerals are left behind. Then they form crystals.

The water in hot springs is heated deep underground. This hot water dissolves minerals from the rocks around it. The minerals break down and mix with the water.

Salt crystals
This picture shows halite (salt) crystals. They formed when seawater evaporated.

The hot water evaporates when it comes to the surface. Crystals can then form. Calcite crystals (see the picture below) often form this way.

Rocks deep inside Earth's **crust** (top layer) are very hot. Water that flows through these rocks dissolves minerals. The water cools as it rises toward Earth's surface. Then the minerals will form crystals. Crystals of gold and galena form this way.

⇐ **These amazing rocks are made of calcite crystals. They formed from hot spring water.**

⇨ **These are gold crystals. They formed as water rose toward Earth's surface.**

crust thin surface layer of Earth

Growth in magma

Crystals form when **magma** (hot liquid rock) cools. It cools underground or at Earth's surface. It forms crystals as it cools. This is known as **crystallization**.

Magma cools slowly underground. There is plenty of time for large crystals to form. This produces rock made up of large crystals. We say that this type of rock is coarse grained.

⇨ **This rock is called pegmatite. It is made up of large crystals.**

crystallization cooling and hardening of hot liquid rock (magma) to form crystals

Sometimes magma rises all the way to Earth's surface. This may be on land or underwater. Then it is called **lava**. Lava comes out of volcanoes.

Lava cools quickly on Earth's surface. There is little time for crystals to grow. The rock produced will have small crystals. We say it is fine grained.

⬅ **This is lava. The lava will quickly cool and harden.**

The wonderful world of geodes

All of the rocks of Earth's **crust** (top layer) are made up of crystals. But large, well-formed crystals are hard to find. The best places to find them are in **cavities** (spaces) in rocks.

Amazing crystals can be found in **geodes**. A geode looks like a normal rock on the outside. But it has a space inside. Beautiful crystals grow in this space.

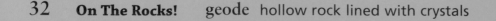

⇩ **This is a geode filled with quartz crystals. Purple quartz is called amethyst.**

Geodes usually form in volcanic areas. **Lava** (hot liquid rock) comes out of volcanoes. It often contains gas bubbles. Gas is a substance like air. Lava hardens to form rock. Sometimes a bubble gets trapped. It forms a cavity in the rock.

Water may become trapped in a cavity. **Minerals** from this water can form crystals. There is space in the cavity for these crystals to grow into large and beautiful shapes.

Geodes and nodules

Geodes are rocks with a hollow space inside.

Nodules are round rocks that are completely packed with small crystals.

⬆ This is a nodule that has been split open. It is packed with beautiful crystals.

ARE ALL CRYSTALS PERFECT?

Crystal cross
Staurolite crystals often grow through one another. This forms cross-shaped crystals, like the ones in this picture.

Crystals do not often have perfect shapes. They can only grow in perfect shapes if they have enough space. Many crystals usually grow in the same place. Then none of them can grow very large.

Small changes can affect a growing crystal. Sometimes a tiny speck of dust can produce strange and wonderful crystals.

Crystals within crystals

Crystals often grow in odd ways. They may look like they are stuck together. One crystal may grow into another one. This is called **twinning**. It often happens in feldspar and gypsum crystals.

Sometimes a crystal will grow on top of a different type of crystal. A crystal can even grow around a smaller one.

Maiden hair
This is a quartz crystal. Needle-shaped crystals have grown inside it. They are called maiden hair.

Crystal impurities

A tiny piece of rock or **mineral** may land on a crystal as it is growing. This piece of rock or mineral is called an **impurity**. It can have a huge effect on the crystal.

Pure quartz crystals are colorless. Sometimes an impurity of iron or aluminum enters the crystal. Then a different colored quartz will be produced.

The blue color of sapphires is caused by impurities. So is the red color of rubies.

amethyst

smoky

clear

rose

milky

impurity   substance that enters a crystal when it is growing

Gypsum crystals may grow in deserts. Grains of sand often get in the way of growing crystals. Then the crystal grows around the sand grains. This produces a growth called desert rose gypsum. Its crystals are flat and look like rose petals.

⬇ **This is desert rose gypsum. Sand grains cause it to grow in a flowerlike shape.**

HOW DO CRYSTALS BREAK UP?

Crystals of the same **mineral** will always break in the same way. The way a crystal breaks is called **cleavage**.

Some crystals break only in one direction. They usually break into flat sheets. Breaking in two directions produces long fragments. Breaking in three or more directions may produce cubes.

The directions of the breaks are called **cleavage planes**. These lines are where the crystal is weakest.

Cleavage planes

one cleavage plane

two cleavage planes

three cleavage planes

Minerals break into different shapes. The shape depends on how many cleavage planes there are.

This is a cubic crystal of galena. It has three cleavage planes. It will break into cubes.

cleavage plane   line of weakness in a mineral, along which the mineral tends to break

Some crystals have no cleavage planes. They break in any direction and into different shapes. Quartz does this. It can break like a pane of glass.

Cutting crystals

Some crystals are cut to be used in jewelry. They are cut along the cleavage planes.

A crystal that is cut across a cleavage plane may shatter.

⬆ These are mica crystals. They have just one cleavage plane. They will break into sheets.

HOW DO WE USE CRYSTALS?

Crystals are very important in everyday life. They have many different uses.

Gemstones in jewelry

Gemstones are crystals that are cut and polished in special ways. This makes them sparkle. Then they are used in jewelry.

The most valuable gemstones are known as precious gemstones. These are the rarest crystals. They are hard to find. They are the hardest crystals. They are also the most beautiful. Rubies, sapphires, and emeralds are all precious gemstones.

Gemstone qualities

A gemstone has three qualities that make it different from other crystals. These are

- rarity
- beauty
- hardness.

⇨ This is a sapphire crystal. Imagine finding a lump of rock with one of these in it!

Diamonds are the most valuable of all gemstones. They are also the hardest. Diamonds are very rare. Most of them are colorless. But **impurities** (see page 36) can make diamonds any color.

Other gemstones are called semiprecious gemstones. These are not as expensive. They include garnet, amethyst, and topaz. Garnet can be a blood-red color. Topaz and amethyst can be many different colors.

The Hope Diamond

The Hope Diamond (pictured below) is very famous. It is a deep blue color. This unusual color comes from impurities in the crystal.

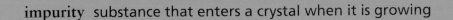

impurity substance that enters a crystal when it is growing

Planes and paint

Most diamonds are not suitable for jewelry. They are too small or have an odd shape. But these diamonds can be used in cutting tools and drills. This is because diamond crystals are very hard.

We use crystals in food. Halite (rock salt) crystals are used as a preservative. A preservative stops food from turning bad. Halite is also used to flavor food.

Rutile crystals contain titanium. This is a very light metal. It is used to make airplanes. It is also used to make white paint.

⇨ **A dentist's drill is made from diamond.**

Quartz crystals are used to make watches (see page 9). Quartz also contains silica. We use it to make silicon chips. There are silicon chips in many electronic items. They are used in computers and coffee makers.

⬇ Halite (salt) is dug out of the ground. Then it is piled up in huge salt mountains, like these. The salt is then left to dry out.

SUMMARY

- Crystals are found in nature. They are solid substances made up of tiny parts called **atoms**.

- The atoms in a crystal are arranged in a special type of pattern. This pattern is called a **lattice**. It gives a crystal its shape. For example, this shape could be a six-sided cube (block).

- Crystals are found in rocks all over Earth. Some are large and beautiful, such as diamonds.

- Crystals form deep inside Earth and at the surface. They form when **magma** (hot melted rock) cools. They also form when water containing minerals **evaporates** (turns into gas).

- We use crystals in many ways. They are in watches and computers. Some are used in jewelry.

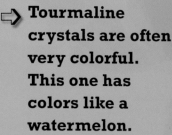
⇨ **Tourmaline crystals are often very colorful. This one has colors like a watermelon.**

FIND OUT MORE

Books

Dickie, Lisa, and Ron Edwards. *Diamonds and Gemstones* (Rocks, Minerals, and Resources). Crabtree Publishing, 2004.

Foa, Emma. *Gemstones* (DK Pockets). New York: DK Children, 2003.

Harding, R. R., and R. F. Symes. *Crystal and Gem* (DK Eyewitness Books). New York: DK, 2007.

Ricciuti, Edward. *Rocks and Minerals* (Scholastic Science Readers). New York: Scholastic, 2002.

Stewart, Melissa. *Crystals* (Rocks & Minerals). Chicago: Heinemann, 2002.

Using the Internet

If you want to find out more about crystals you can search the Internet. Try using keywords such as these:

- geode
- crystallography
- diamond.

You can also use different keywords. Try choosing some words from this book.

Try using a search directory such as www.yahooligans.com

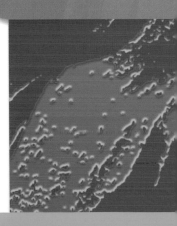

GLOSSARY

atom tiny particle that elements and minerals are made from

cavity hollow or space inside something

cleavage the way a mineral breaks

cleavage plane line of weakness in a mineral, along which the mineral tends to break

core center of Earth

crust thin surface layer of Earth

crystal face flat side of a crystal

crystal habit way that crystals grow and fit together

crystal system one of six groups that crystals are divided into

crystallization cooling and hardening of hot liquid rock (magma) to form crystals

crystallographer scientist who studies crystals

erosion wearing away and removal of weathered rock

evaporate turn into a gas

gemstone crystal that is cut and polished for use in jewelry

geode hollow rock lined with crystals

igneous rock rock formed from magma either underground or at Earth's surface

impurity substance that enters a crystal when it is growing

lattice three-dimensional pattern or arrangement. Three-dimensional means it has length, width, and depth.

lava name for magma when it reaches the surface of Earth

magma melted rock from Earth's mantle

mantle hot layer of Earth beneath the crust

metamorphic rock rock formed when igneous or sedimentary rocks are changed by heat or pressure

microscope device used to see very small objects. It makes them appear bigger.

mineral substance found in nature. Rocks are made from lots of minerals.

nodule round rock completely filled with small crystals

polymorph minerals that contain the same atoms, but have their atoms arranged in different ways

pressure weight or force pressing against something

pyramid shape with a square base and sloping triangles. The triangles meet together in a point.

rock cycle unending cycle of rock formation and destruction

sediment pieces of rock that have been worn away and moved to another place

sedimentary rock rock formed from the broken pieces of other rocks

twinning when two crystals grow into or through one another

weathering breaking down of rock

INDEX

48